TWA
Flight 800

Titles in the *American Disasters* series:

The Exxon Valdez
Tragic Oil Spill
ISBN 0-7660-1058-9

Hurricane Andrew
Nature's Rage
ISBN 0-7660-1057-0

The L.A. Riots
Rage in the City of Angels
ISBN 0-7660-1219-0

The Mighty Midwest Flood
Raging Rivers
ISBN 0-7660-1221-2

The Oklahoma City Bombing
Terror in the Heartland
ISBN 0-7660-1061-9

Plains Outbreak Tornadoes
Killer Twisters
ISBN 0-7660-1059-7

San Francisco Earthquake, 1989
Death and Destruction
ISBN 0-7660-1060-0

The Siege at Waco
Deadly Inferno
ISBN 0-7660-1218-2

The World Trade Center Bombing
Terror in the Towers
ISBN 0-7660-1056-2

TWA Flight 800

Explosion in Midair

Michael D. Cole

Enslow Publishers, Inc.

44 Hadem Road   PO Box 38
Box 699   Aldershot
Springfield, NJ 07081   Hants GU12 6BP
USA   UK

http://www.enslow.com

Library of Congress Cataloging-in-Publication Data

Cole, Michael D.
    TWA flight 800 : explosion in midair / Michael D. Cole
       p.   cm. — (American Disasters)
    Includes bibliographical references and index.
    Summary: Describes the explosion that caused TWA Flight 800 to break apart in
midair, killing 230 people on July 17, 1996, and examines some possible causes for
the disaster.
    ISBN 0-7660-1217-4
    1. Aircraft accidents—New York (State)—Long Island Region— Juvenile
literature. [Aircraft accidents.] I. Title. II. Series.
TL553.5.C517   1999
363.12'465'0974721—dc21   98-30265
                                                  CIP
                                                    AC

Printed in the United States of America

10 9 8 7 6 5 4 3 2 1

To Our Readers:
All Internet addresses in this book were active and appropriate when we went to press.
Any comments or suggestions can be sent by e-mail to Comments@enslow.com or to
the address on the back cover.

Photo Credits: AP/Wide World Photos, pp. 1, 6, 8, 9, 10, 15, 17, 18, 20, 25, 26,
27, 32, 33, 35, 38, 40, 41, 42, 43; shown on p. 20: Michel Breistroff, father of
the victim of the same name; shown on p. 38: three Montoursville High School
girls. © Corel Corporation, shown on p. 6: The Eiffel Tower, Paris, France.

Cover Photo: AP/Wide World Photos

Contents

CHAPTER 1

Cleared for Takeoff

The giant Boeing 747 airliner backed away from its gate at New York's John F. Kennedy International Airport. The time was shortly after 8 P.M. on July 17, 1996. As flight attendants prepared the cabin for takeoff, the 212 passengers aboard Trans World Airlines (TWA) Flight 800 settled in for their flight.

Many of them relaxed and fastened their seat belts as the aircraft taxied to runway 22R. The plane lined up behind a few other planes on the runway. In the cockpit, Captain Steven Snyder and First Officer Ralph Kevorkian awaited Flight 800's clearance for takeoff.

Minutes later the control tower gave clearance to Flight 800. The crew acknowledged clearance, and Captain Snyder pushed the throttle forward to accelerate the 747's engines. The plane's speed increased rapidly as it roared down the runway. Captain Snyder pulled back easily on the wheel, and at 8:19 P.M. TWA Flight 800 took off into the evening sky.

The passengers aboard Flight 800 were bound for

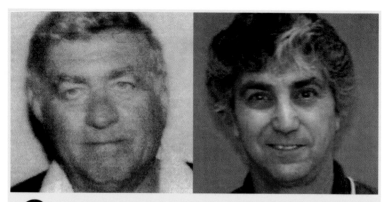

*C*aptain Stephen Snyder (left) and First Officer Ralph Kevorkian commanded the cockpit of TWA Flight 800.

Paris, France. Some of the passengers were headed there on business. Some were going for a vacation. One group of high school students was going on an educational trip. Sixteen members of the high school French club, along with their teacher and four other chaperones, were traveling to Paris to learn about the French language and culture. The students and their chaperones were from the small town of Montoursville, Pennsylvania.

These young people were just beginning to settle in as the plane gained altitude for the long flight. Whatever they were planning to do to pass the next eight hours would barely get started. The same would turn out to be true for all the other passengers.

The plane continued to climb toward fourteen thousand feet, flying east over the Atlantic Ocean. Within minutes, it was more than ten miles east of the southern

*V*ictims Eric and Virginia Holst had planned to celebrate their sixth wedding anniversary in Paris, France.

shore of Long Island. At 8:25 P.M., New York air traffic control switched the monitoring of the flight over to Boston air traffic control.

Eric and Virginia Holst were seated aboard the plane. The couple was going to France to attend the wedding of Eric's brother. They also planned to celebrate their own sixth wedding anniversary the following day in Paris.[1] They would never get to celebrate that anniversary. They would not make it to Paris.

Neither would TWA flight attendant

*M*onica Michelle Weaver was one of the students from Montoursville, Penn.

*G*race Melotin was a flight attendant on the ill-fated TWA Flight 800. She is seen here in uniform in this undated family photo.

Rosemary Braman-Mosberg. Braman-Mosberg loved her work as a flight attendant. She had not originally been scheduled to be on the New York to Paris flight, but had been added to the crew of Flight 800 at the last minute.[2]

It would also be the final voyage for flight attendant Grace Melotin. She had just turned forty-eight years old.

The flight attendants, Captain Snyder, First Officer Kevorkian, Eric and Virginia Holst, the teenagers from Montoursville, and everyone else aboard the aircraft had no idea what was about to happen to their flight.

CHAPTER 2

Fireball

The aircraft continued to climb. Boston air traffic control gave clearance for the plane to climb to fifteen thousand feet. It was at thirteen thousand feet and still climbing. Instruments in the cockpit indicated to the crew that everything aboard the plane was fine. Boston air traffic controllers monitored the path of Flight 800 on radar as it continued outward over the Atlantic Ocean.

Suddenly the unthinkable happened.

At 8:32 P.M., a terrible explosion ripped through the interior of the aircraft. The blast tore away a section of the fuselage, the long part of the plane containing the passengers. With this sudden gaping hole in the aircraft, the plane's cabin quickly lost pressure. Loose articles began flying violently through the cabin and were sucked out through the opening.

Worse, the powerful explosion had also broken the aircraft's keel beam, the steel spine that runs the length of a plane. With the keel beam broken, there was nothing left to hold the length of the aircraft together.

Seconds after the explosion, the nose of the aircraft broke off from the rest of the plane just ahead of where the wings joined the fuselage. The cockpit with Captain Snyder and First Officer Kevorkian and the forward part of the aircraft with about one hundred passengers fell helplessly toward the water.

Blunt and broken, the rest of the plane tilted upward, spilling below it a trail of flaming jet fuel into the air. All four engines continued to function. A few moments later the tremendous forces being exerted on the opened aircraft caused the fuel tank in the plane's right wing to burst open. This tank was full, and as hundreds of gallons of fuel suddenly hit the air, they mingled with the flames trailing from the blunt end of the broken plane. Then the flames ignited the fuel, causing a huge explosion.[1]

The back part of the aircraft, engulfed in a giant fireball, was so bright that it was seen for miles away up and down the southern coast of Long Island.

The shattered Boeing 747, with all 230 passengers and crew aboard, plunged into the chilly waters of the Atlantic Ocean, two miles below.

All of this happened very quickly and very close to sunset. The fact that darkness was falling made the exploding fireball all the more visible in the sky. Many people witnessed the distant explosion from points along the southern coastline of Long Island. Chris Baur witnessed it from the air.

Baur was a helicopter pilot with the New York Air National Guard. He was piloting his HH-60 helicopter during a routine training mission with the 106th Rescue Wing when he saw the fireball in the sky.

Baur saw two explosions, then what he described as "a waterfall of flames" spiraling down toward the water.[2] Baur's flight engineer, Dennis Richardson, saw it too. He hung on as Baur immediately swung his helicopter south, toward the direction of the flames.

"Maybe two planes had collided," Baur thought, as he throttled the helicopter to maximum power, flying down to a spot where flames were leaping fifty feet into the air.[3] Glowing ashes were still falling downward. Through the smoke and the ashes, Baur saw what he thought was a young man in blue jeans and a T-shirt floating face down in the water amid the wreckage. A year earlier, Baur had won a medal of valor for rescuing three stranded fishermen. He wondered whether he was about to rescue someone again.

"I thought, if he's alive, I could at least get his face out of the water and keep him afloat," Baur later said.[4] But there was no movement. As darkness continued to fall, Baur saw through the dimness that the man in the T-shirt was floating lifelessly in the water. Baur and Richardson had only begun to discover the horror of the scene around them.

"I've got a body!" Richardson shouted suddenly. A closer look revealed to him that there were actually several bodies. As Bauer kept the helicopter hovering over the water, Richardson spotted several more. A little farther on, he saw twenty or more bodies clumped together in the water.[5]

The two men could see that something terrible had happened. A disaster. But what kind of disaster could have occurred?

Then Baur's headset crackled with the awful news. A 747 had disappeared from radar somewhere off the southern coast of Long Island. A 747, one of the largest commercial planes in operation, had exploded and gone down over the ocean. Baur and Richardson were seeing only part of the wreckage. There was much more out there in the growing darkness.

It was just after 9 P.M. when James Kallstrom's beeper went off inside the restaurant where he had just finished eating dinner. As assistant director of the Federal Bureau of Investigation (FBI), Kallstrom was head of the FBI's 24-hour electronic command post in New York City. He pulled out his cellular phone.

A special agent monitoring the command post informed Kallstrom that a Boeing 747 had disappeared from air-traffic controllers' radar screens. The agent added that there had been no communications about any emergency from the flight crew, and no sign of trouble with the flight. It had simply vanished from the screen.[6]

Kallstrom put the cellular phone away. He knew that the Boeing 747 was a big plane with a good safety record. He was not aware that any 747 had ever crashed because of mechanical failure. It would take something very powerful to knock the huge aircraft out of the sky.[7]

*J*ames Kallstrom, assistant director of the FBI, would soon find himself in charge of the investigation of the Flight 800 disaster.

Kallstrom would soon find himself in charge of a long FBI investigation into the cause of the crash. He and others in the FBI were not in the habit of voicing their own ideas about what had happened before they looked at all the facts. Yet among many of the government officials, rescue workers, and investigators who became involved in the disaster's aftermath that night, there was a common suspicion that an act of terrorism had taken place.

The beginning of the 1996 Olympic Games in Atlanta, Georgia, was only days away. Because of the worldwide attention focused on the games, they were commonly viewed as a likely target for terrorist activity. Tight security was crucial there. Whatever had happened to Flight 800, the fact that it had gone down so close to the opening of the Olympic Games made the crash even more disturbing. To many people, it did not seem that the timing of the disaster could be a coincidence.

The terrible news flashed across Jim Cullen's television set. The bulletin reported that the plane had gone down ten miles off Moriches Inlet, near the area on Long Island where Cullen lived. Moments later his phone rang. It was his neighbor, Mike O'Reilly.

"Did you hear about it?" O'Reilly asked.

"Let's go," Cullen replied.[8]

O'Reilly owned a powerful speedboat that could do fifty-five miles per hour on the water. The two men met at the dock and hopped aboard O'Reilly's boat. Within a short time they were headed out into the inlet. By then, it was completely dark. There was no moon. The winds were light and the sea calm. But there was nothing calm about the scene they saw beyond the inlet.

A few miles out, the area was lit up with flames, the sparkling of flares, and the glare of hovering rescue helicopter lights. Cullen and O'Reilly pushed their speeding boat to full throttle, hoping to reach the wreckage and save any survivors they might find floating in the water. Several Coast Guard, fishing, and other weekend pleasure boats had already gathered around the scene of the tragedy. Like Cullen and O'Reilly, they were hoping to find survivors.

They would find none.

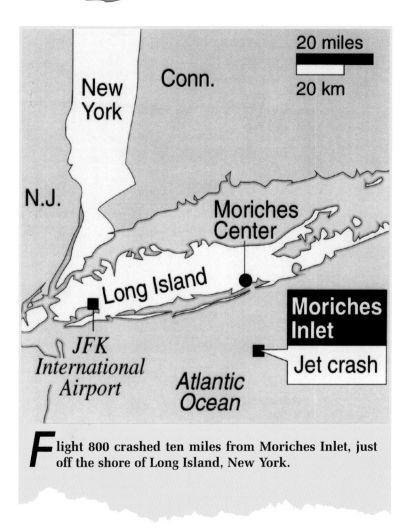

*F*light 800 crashed ten miles from Moriches Inlet, just off the shore of Long Island, New York.

What they found instead was a horrible scene of death and destruction. The plane had been torn to pieces so violently that no one could have survived.

"There were legs and internal parts floating around," Cullen said. The scene of destruction around them was a sight that Cullen described as pure "hell."[9]

Hours later, the two men made their way slowly back

*O*ne of the many pieces of the Boeing 747 that was found in the cold waters of the Atlantic Ocean.

across the water. Their sleek and sporty boat was now loaded with a grotesque cargo of twisted bodies. At 4:30 A.M., after docking their boat, Cullen and O'Reilly went through the process of turning the bodies over to police.

At the end of that terrible night, which was actually early in the morning of July 18, the two men went home.

"How was it?" Cullen's wife Linda asked, when he arrived back home.

"You don't want to know," he replied.[10]

The recovery of bodies from the wreckage was far from finished. Many of them were trapped beneath the water amid parts of the plane's wreckage. As bodies continued to be recovered throughout the night, the families of those who had just perished aboard TWA Flight 800 were beginning to learn the awful news.

CHAPTER 3

The Terrible Loss

There's been a crash," said Aurelie Becker's mother-in-law on the phone. Aurelie's daughter, Michele, and her college friend Becky Olsen had been scheduled to fly to Paris that night. As her mother-in-law asked what plane Michele was on, Becker felt a chill.[1] She knew the number of her daughter's scheduled flight, but she was also aware that international flights are often overbooked. Aurelie Becker hoped and prayed that her daughter had gotten bumped to a later flight.

Quickly, Becker gathered the paperwork on her daughter's flight and sat down with her husband, Walter, to watch the bulletins about the flight on television news station CNN. Later, Becker and her other daughter, Katy, drove twenty-five miles to the airport in Tampa, Florida. The people at the TWA desk tried to help but could give them no information about Flight 800's passenger list. They returned home and continued to wait through a sleepless night.

At 10 A.M. the next morning, Becker got a call from her brother, John Bogensberger, who lived on Long Island. He had been to the beach where the rescue operations were being conducted. He had spoken to someone who told him that Michele and Becky's names were not on the passenger roster.

Unfortunately, the Beckers' relief was very short-lived.

Soon Becker's brother called again with news of an updated passenger list. This time Michele's and Becky's names were on it.

"I felt," Becker said, "as if everything in my whole heart and soul just sank."[2]

TWA arranged to fly the Beckers to New York. It was the beginning of a long ordeal of grieving for the Becker family. They were not alone.

The process of gathering the families had already begun, even before Walter and Aurelie Becker had learned the terrible news of their daughter's death. From all across the United States, from France, and from other countries, TWA began making preparations to fly into New York the families and friends of those lost aboard Flight 800.

Earlier that morning, at 7 A.M. on the day after the crash, New York governor George Pataki was in a helicopter hovering over the crash area. As terrible as it was to be viewing the crash site, Pataki dreaded the job ahead of him even more. He would soon meet with some of the victims' families to try to console them.[3]

Pataki went to JFK airport's Ramada Plaza Hotel where the families TWA had already flown in were staying.

These were the families who had found out the earliest. It had been a long and nightmarish night for them. In one of the hotel's ballrooms, some of these family members were huddled in blankets.

Some of the victims' families hugged the governor and thanked him for coming. Others wept. Some just stared vacantly into space, still in shock from the sudden tragedy. A few of the families asked the governor whether they could travel to the scene of the crash, but Pataki discouraged this action. He had been told by experts that a close-up experience would only worsen their grief.

The families were crying and asking why. In a scene of such terrible tragedy, the governor could no longer bottle up his emotions. Pataki's own daughter was eleven years old. He could not help thinking of her as he witnessed the grief of those parents. He could not help thinking how he would feel if his own daughter had been on that plane. After a few moments, Governor Pataki broke down and cried with the victims' families.[4]

Later that evening, Walter and Aurelie Becker arrived at the Ramada. It was going to be a long and terrible wait for many families. It would take days and even weeks for some of the bodies to be found. Then, because of the violent nature of the crash and the amount of time they had been under water, many of the bodies were in very bad condition. Once they were recovered, it took medical examiners a long time to identify them.

"It seemed the search parties would never find Michele," Becker said. "So on July 22, five days after the crash, we had a memorial service for her. We put up a picture of her with one of the teddy bears the Red Cross had donated."[5]

Each day, more of the families waiting at the hotel were called and told that their loved ones' remains had been identified. After having been recovered from the seas by Navy divers, the remains were identified by police and medical examiners from dental records and finger-prints. The divers were not only recovering bodies, but also helping to recover sunken parts of the plane, from large sections of the fuselage to smaller bits of wreckage. This operation turned out to be the first phase of the investigation into the cause of the crash.

"We were very conscious of the fact that grieving fam-ilies were waiting on shore to see if their loved ones would be found," said Lieutenant Commander Bill Orr, commanding officer of the USS *Grasp*.[6] The *Grasp* was a Navy ship designed for diving and recovery operations.

"Oddly enough, seeing personal effects, such as pass-ports or wallets with family photos, affected us more deeply than the remains themselves," Orr recalled. "We had a job to do. Divers were visibly upset if they had to come topside without finding anyone. Those who recov-ered victims were visibly relieved that at least one more family had a loved one back."[7]

What remained of the plane was scattered along a five-mile path beneath one hundred twenty feet of water. Two important pieces of the plane to find were the flight data box and the cockpit voice recorder, the so-called "black box." This device is actually colored bright orange so it can be found easily after a crash.

The flight data box is an electronic machine that records information about the plane's performance during a flight. It also records what position all the switches in the cockpit were in throughout the flight. The cockpit voice recorder records all voices and sounds made in the

*T*he USS *Grasp* is a Navy ship designed for diving and recovery operations. It was used to search for bodies of the victims and pieces of wreckage from the TWA airplane.

*A*ll of the Navy divers needed lights to see in the murky midnight waters.

cockpit during the flight. Finding these two boxes could give investigators important clues about what had happened aboard the plane before the explosion.

Late on the evening of July 25, eight days after the crash, two of the *Grasp*'s Navy divers went into the water for their second dive. The divers wore hard diving helmets with lights attached to them. The diving helmets were equipped with microphones so the divers could communicate with the ship. It was ten minutes before midnight. Their lights barely cut through the deep blackness of the sea around them.

They walked along the bottom of the sea, sweeping their lights through the dark water, thick with plankton and schools of baitfish. Up ahead a brown object suddenly turned bright orange when caught in the divers' lights. Moments later, their lights swept over another orange box lying nearby.

"We have them," said one of the divers into his

*T*he flight data box and cockpit voice recorder are displayed. They received only moderate damage in the crash and held clues about the cause of the disaster.

microphone. "We've got the flight data and cockpit voice recorders."[8]

There was a short cheer and a small gasp of relief from the people on the ship above. The divers had found two of the most important pieces of the wreck. These might greatly aid the investigation. The families of the victims, the FBI, the people at TWA, and the rest of the public wanted to know what had brought the huge plane down.

Specifically, they wanted to know whether a bomb had exploded aboard TWA Flight 800. The investigation by the

FBI and the National Transportation and Safety Board (NTSB) was well under way, even before all of the victims' bodies were recovered.

By August 2, the body of Walter and Aurelie Becker's daughter had yet to be found. The Beckers had been staying at the airport's Ramada Hotel since the day after the crash. Walter was still trying to convince Aurelie that they needed to go home. Only a few families were left whose loved ones' remains had yet to be found.

On the following day, August 3, the Beckers received a message from TWA.

"I have news," the TWA representative said. Aurelie Becker knew her daughter had been found. It turned out that Michele's body had been recovered on the same day divers had discovered the pilot in the cockpit.[9]

Medical examiners had identified Michele by dental X rays and fingerprints. They had also found a ring on the second toe of her left foot. Michele Becker had wanted to get a tattoo. When her mother discouraged it, Michele decided instead to wear a silver ring on her toe. Michele wore it "just to be different," Becker said.[10]

By now, the remains of most victims and the majority of the pieces of the plane's wreckage had been recovered from the crash area. For many people, however, the tragedy of TWA Flight 800 was far from over. Indeed, the families' grieving and the government's investigation into the crash were only beginning.

CHAPTER 4

The Mystery of Flight 800

What caused TWA Flight 800 to go down?

Finding the answer to that question was the job of the FBI and the NTSB. FBI investigators, led by James Kallstrom, looked for clues and followed any evidence that suggested a criminal act might have brought the plane down. The NTSB investigators went about the process of piecing the plane back together. Experts at the NTSB made many technical studies of the recovered wreckage parts to find out exactly what had happened to the plane.

Kallstrom and his FBI investigators had their hands full. There were theories that a bomb had been placed on the plane and had exploded during the flight. Early on, there was no evidence of such a bomb.

Many witnesses who had seen the explosion from along the Long Island coast claimed they had seen something streaking upward toward the plane before it exploded. News of what these witnesses had seen caused some people to believe that terrorists had shot a shoulder-fired missile at the plane.

Another theory had to do with the fact that U.S. Navy ships had been on maneuvers near the area of the crash. The presence of naval ships in the area, combined with the witnesses' claims of seeing a missile, made some people suspect that a U.S. Navy missile might have accidentally hit the Boeing 747 and caused it to explode.

Kallstrom and his FBI agents pursued all these possibilities. There was a chance that a bomb might have been placed aboard the plane while it was at the Hellinikon Airport in Athens, Greece. The Boeing 747 had taken off from Athens before landing in New York. Despite the fact that the Hellinikon Airport had been a target for terrorists in the past, its security was still rather weak.[1] Yet it appeared that nothing unusual had happened at Athens. The plane had landed and unloaded its passengers and baggage. The plane was checked out and reloaded for the New York flight, and took off without incident.

FBI investigators could find no evidence of suspicious passengers or ground crew members who might have taken or placed a bomb aboard the plane. Investigators for the NTSB also found no evidence of a bomb explosion in the recovered wreckage of the aircraft.

The evidence NTSB investigators were studying indicated that an explosion had somehow occurred in the aircraft's center fuel tank. The most badly burned and charred pieces of the plane were located near the area of this fuel tank. If there was no bomb, investigators' next question was, what kind of mechanical failure would have caused such a terrible explosion in the nearly empty fuel tank?

By August 30, six weeks after the crash, some dramatic new evidence had emerged. NTSB investigators had discovered something on a few pieces of the recovered wreckage. They had found small traces of chemicals called PETN and RDX. Both the PETN and RDX chemicals were used in the making of plastic explosives.

This discovery changed everything. Traces of explosives had been found among the wreckage of the plane.

Investigators immediately went to work finding out how the explosives could have gotten aboard the aircraft. They explored every possibility, including checking sources of explosives other than from a bomb. After weeks of searching for clues, the investigators found some answers while looking into a certain regular Federal Aviation Administration (FAA) procedure.

The FAA oversees and regulates all matters of aviation in the United States. One of its safety regulations requires that the abilities of bomb-sniffing dogs be tested regularly. It was discovered that such a test had been conducted aboard the TWA Boeing 747. On June 10, 1996, in St. Louis, Missouri, police had used this aircraft to test bomb-sniffing dogs of the St. Louis police canine unit. Packets of PETN and RDX had been hidden in the aircraft for this test and removed afterward, but the residue from these chemicals remained in the plane. This chemical residue from the bomb-sniffing test was what had been detected by the investigators.[2]

*A*dog checks for chemicals at Boston's Logan Airport. The TWA Boeing 747 had been used earlier to conduct tests with similar bomb-sniffing dogs.

The FBI and the NTSB were now right back where they started, without any real evidence of a bomb. The only evidence they had of a missile was the description of a streak of flame given by several witnesses. All the hard evidence still pointed to an explosion in the aircraft's center fuel tank.

Two months after the tragedy, the recovered pieces of the Boeing 747 were laid out on the floor of a large airplane hangar in Calverton, Long Island. Al Dickinson, NTSB's investigator-in-charge for Flight 800, was looking at where the pieces of the center fuel tank had been carefully arranged.

"There were pieces that had soot and fire damage, the kinds of things you'd expect in a major explosion," Dickinson said. "No other area of the aircraft had this kind of damage and destruction."[3]

It was then that NTSB investigators decided to build a full, three-dimensional reconstruction of the fuselage, both ahead of and behind the area where the center fuel tank had exploded. In all, nearly ninety feet of the fuselage would be reassembled from the wreckage. It would be

A large section of fuselage from the 747 is loaded onto a flatbed truck to be taken to the hangar in Calverton, Long Island.

the largest reconstruction of a wrecked aircraft ever attempted. Pieces of the wreckage were still coming in.

By the beginning of November, Navy divers had spent fifteen weeks searching the ocean floor for wreckage. Two days after the divers were finished, fishing trawlers began scraping the bottom for any remaining pieces of the aircraft.

The year 1997 arrived with little news about the cause of the crash of Flight 800. On February 8, victims' families were allowed to tour the wreckage assembled at the hangar. By then, much of the wreckage from the interior of the plane was arranged on a grid. Investigators had placed the battered passenger seats in rows, just as they had been inside the aircraft. The site of the wreckage laid out across the hangar was a striking scene for the families. They walked through the wreckage slowly and quietly. Many of them placed roses on the seats where their loved ones had spent their last moments alive.

Months went by as investigators continued to study and reconstruct the wreckage. Roy Hurlbut is an aeronautical engineer who assisted in the reconstruction. He said working with the thousands of pieces of wreckage was frustrating at times.

"When your time on site turns into several months, it can take a toll on you," Hurlbut said. "All you can do is keep your eye on the goal, which is to figure out what happened. Because you don't want it to happen again. That's what keeps you going."[4]

By the end of April, more than 95 percent of the aircraft had been recovered from the water. On May 18,

1997, the NTSB officially ended the search for the debris. Ten months after the crash, investigators had all the pieces of wreckage they were going to get. After this massive investigation by both the FBI and the Central Intelligence Agency (CIA), there was absolutely no sign that a bomb or missile had caused the plane to go down.

Joe Lychner, who lost his wife and two daughters in the crash, walks among the recovered wreckage of the ill-fated flight almost a year later.

All evidence still pointed to an explosion in the aircraft's center fuel tank.

As the investigation became increasingly focused on the center fuel tank, the three-dimensional reconstruction of the fuselage was fully under way. A huge framework of metal ribs was welded together to support the large pieces of wreckage. After a worker noted that the framework resembled the ribs of a large animal, it was christened "Jetosaurus Rex."[5]

On June 9, 1997, victims' families were informed that the investigation was in its final phases. Despite the efforts of the FBI and the CIA, no evidence had been found of a criminal act. The NTSB officially blamed the disaster on a center fuel tank explosion. Investigators were still trying to determine the details of what exactly had caused that explosion.

In July 1997, the NTSB flew a series of test flights. A Boeing 747 was equipped with computers and one hundred fifty different sensors in an effort to help determine the conditions that might have caused the explosion.[6] These tests, and work in other areas of the investigation, were pointing investigators toward the possibility that faulty wiring inside the fuel tank had caused the disaster. The NTSB believed that a spark or an arc of electricity between corroded wires might have ignited the fuel vapors within the tank, resulting in an explosion.[7]

Witnesses still claimed they had seen what looked like the trail of a missile just before the plane exploded. But a careful description of crash events explained the trail of fire they saw streaking though the sky on the night of July 17, 1996.

In the growing dimness of twilight, the center fuel tank explosion blew away the front part of the fuselage. In the moments that followed, burning fuel leaked in a downward stream from the plane, as the back part of the aircraft climbed higher through the sky. It is likely that this trail of flame looked like something streaking upward to meet what, seconds later, was the final explosion, which shattered the rest of the aircraft.

"The relief, if there is any, comes from the fact that 230 people did not die because someone wanted them to," said Jose Cremades of Strasbourg, France. He had lost his sixteen-year-old son Daniel on Flight 800.[8]

Still mourning the loss of her daughter Michele, Aurelie Becker said, "My fear right now is that if this is not a terrorist act it could happen again today, tomorrow, to anybody."[9]

Concern for the safety of all who fly commercial planes is why chairman Jim Hall said the NTSB would continue to follow any new leads that might give answers to what had caused the Flight 800 tragedy.

"We owe it to the American people," he said.[10]

As of mid-1998, no new information had been uncovered. The exact cause of the explosion aboard TWA Flight 800 remains a mystery.

CHAPTER 5

Painful
Anniversary

One year after the crash of TWA Flight 800, victims' families looked back at a very painful event in their lives. For most of them, the emotional wounds were only beginning to heal.

On the beach at Smith Point Park, Long Island, near where the plane went down, the families of victims gathered on July 17, 1997. It was the first anniversary of the crash. Officials involved in the tragedy's aftermath and investigation were also present.

"The sea behind me has claimed a piece of your hearts and a lifetime of your tears," said New York governor George Pataki, again on hand to try to console the families. "Something in your heart will always draw back to this sacred place. You have gathered to observe a dark day in history."[1] The names of the victims were read aloud. After the ceremony, families walked to the shoreline and placed roses in the sand or threw them in the water.

Joe Lychner, who lost his wife and two daughters in

the crash, was with the other families that day at the seaside memorial. "This day is very unsettling," he said. "As the hour [of the crash] draws closer, it becomes more and more unbearable."[2]

*O*n July 17, 1997, the first anniversary of the crash, Governor George Pataki (second from left) places a wreath in a boat at a memorial service held for victims of Flight 800.

*M*ichel Breistroff's girlfriend, Heidi Snow, had agreed to marry him shortly before he climbed aboard Flight 800.

One of the largest groups of mourners at the memorial was the family of Michel Breistroff from Roubaix, France. Breistroff was a recent graduate of Harvard University and was a member of the French Olympic hockey team.

One year earlier he had stopped at a pay phone in Terminal 5 of JFK Airport to call his girlfriend, Heidi Snow.

*F*amilies of the victims testified before the National Transportation Safety Board (NTSB) in favor of stricter safety regulations for air travel.

It was an important call. He had phoned Heidi to ask her if she would marry him. She had said yes.

After saying their goodbyes, Breistroff hung up the phone, picked up his bags, and got in line with the other passengers waiting to board TWA Flight 800.

Neither his new fiancée nor his family would ever see or hear from Breistroff again.

"There is no solution and no answer," said Heidi Snow after the anniversary ceremony. "But at least we can try to help each other."[3]

The victims' families have indeed helped each other through their grief.

"Most of all, my work with the other families has saved me," said Aurelie Becker. "Our friends and neighbors who haven't been through it just don't understand. When you get together with others who have had the same experiences, you know you're not crazy."[4]

The families have also testified before congressional committees to push for better air-safety regulations.

"It's better to think that a mechanical failure was to blame," Becker added. "But it also makes us all the more determined to press for additional air-safety measures, so the rest of the flying public will be protected, and the people who died on Flight 800 will not have died in vain."[5]

A toy bunny and other items sit under the boardwalk at Smith Point Park after the memorial service.

Lessons are sometimes learned in tragedies. Perhaps better safety measures and safer planes will rise from the smoke and ashes of this disaster.

It would be a fitting memorial to the 230 people who tragically lost their lives in the crash of TWA Flight 800.

Chapter Notes

Chapter 1. Cleared for Takeoff

1. Stuart Vincent, *Newsday*, "Their Anniversary Trip Was Going to Be Special," special section compilation, August 1996, <http://www.newsday.com/jet/jetbio1.htm> (September 8, 1998).

2. Fred Bruning, *Newsday*, "The Victims of Flight 800," special section compilation, August 1996, <http://www.newsday.com/jet/jetbio1.htm> (September 8, 1998).

Chapter 2. Fireball

1. Lauren Terrazzano, *Newsday*, "Missile Theory Jettisoned: Flight 800 Report Favors Trail of Fuel," October 1, 1997, <http://www.newsday.com/jet/year/cras1001.htm> (September 8, 1998).

2. Evan Thomas, *Newsweek*, "Death on Flight 800," July 29, 1996, p. 30.

3. Ibid.

4. Ibid.

5. Ibid.

6. Brian Duffy, *U.S. News and World Report*, "Clues from the Sky," July 29, 1996, pp. 22–23.

7. Ibid.

8. Thomas, p. 30.

9. Ibid.

10. Ibid.

Chapter 3. The Terrible Loss

1. Aurelie Becker and Francine Russo, *McCall's*, "Life After Flight 800: In Memory of Michele," August 1997, pp. 68–70.

2. Ibid.

3. Evan Thomas, *Newsweek*, "Death on Flight 800," July 29, 1996, pp. 30–31.

4. Ibid.

5. Becker and Russo, p. 70.

6. Tom Morrisey, *Scuba Times*, "The Recovery of TWA Flight 800: Dissecting the Disaster," March/April 1997, p. 67.

7. Ibid., pp. 67–68.

8. Ibid., p. 66.

9. Becker and Russo, p. 72.

10. Ibid.

Chapter 4. The Mystery of Flight 800

1. Evan Thomas, *Newsweek*, "Death on Flight 800," July 29, 1996, p. 33.

2. Kevin Fedarko, *Time*, "A Theory Gone to the Dogs," September 30, 1996, p. 32.

3. William Triplett, *Air & Space*, "The Reconstruction," August/September 1997, p. 25.

4. Ibid., p. 27.

5. Ibid., p. 29.

6. Sylvia Adcock, *Newsday*, "Testing the Fatal Flight," July 15, 1997, <http://www.newsday.com/jet/year/test 0715.htm> (September 8, 1998).

7. Sylvia Adcock and Laura Terrazzano, *Newsday*, "Down to the Wire," November 13, 1997, <http://www.newsday.com/jet/year/cras1113.htm> (September 8, 1998).

8. Paul Hoversten, *USA Today*, "TWA Families Take Little Comfort," November 19, 1997, p. 3A.

9. Ibid.

10. Ibid.

Chapter 5. Painful Anniversary

1. Pat Milton, *Associated Press*, "TWA 800 Victims Remembered," July 18, 1997, <http://www.newsday.com/ap/rnmpg41g.htm> (November 1997).

2. Ibid.

3. Ibid.

4. Aurelie Becker and Francine Russo, *McCall's*, "Life After Flight 800: In Memory of Michele," August 1997, p. 72.

5. Ibid.

Federal Aviation Administration (FAA)—The United States government agency that regulates private and commercial flights.

Federal Bureau of Investigation (FBI)—The United States government agency in charge of investigating criminal activities within United States borders.

fuselage—The central body of an airplane. It carries the crew and passengers or cargo.

medical examiner—A doctor who examines bodies after death to find the cause of death.

National Transportation Safety Board (NTSB)—The United States government agency that investigates airplane accidents and all major railroad, highway, and boat accidents. Based on these investigations, the NTSB also makes safety recommendations.

terrorists—People who use acts of violence such as bombings or hijackings to try to achieve their political goals or to gain attention for their political causes.

Articles

Becker, Aurelie, and Francine Russo, "Life After Flight 800: In Memory of Michele," McCall's, August 1997, pp. 66–69.

Duffy, Brian, "Clues from the Sky," *U.S. News and World Report*, July 29, 1996, pp. 22–27.

Fedarko, Kevin, "A Theory Gone to the Dogs," *Time*, September 30, 1996, p. 32.

Hoversten, Paul, "TWA Families Take Little Comfort," *USA Today*, November 19, 1997, p. 3A.

Morrisey, Tom, "The Recovery of TWA Flight 800: Dissecting the Disaster," *Scuba Times*, March/April 1997, pp. 66–69.

Thomas, Evan, "Death on Flight 800," *Newsweek*, July 29, 1996, pp. 26–33.

Thomas, Evan and Mark Hosenball, "Death on Flight III," *Newsweek*, September 14, 1998, pp. 22–27.

Triplett, William, "The Reconstruction," *Air & Space*, August/ September 1997, pp. 23–30.

Internet Addresses

Adcock, Sylvia, "Testing the Fatal Flight," Newsday, July 15, 1997, <http://www.newsday.com/jet/year/test0715.htm> (September 8, 1998).

Adcock, Sylvia, and Laura Terrazzano, "Down to the Wire," *Newsday*, November 13, 1997, <http://www.newsday.com/jet/year/cras1113.htm> (September 8, 1998).

Bruning, Fred, "The Victims of Flight 800," *Newsday* special section compilation, August 1996, <http://www.newsday.com/jet/jetbio1.htm> (September 8, 1998).

Terrazzano, Lauren, "Missile Theory Jettisoned: Flight 800 Report Favors Trail of Fuel," *Newsday*, October 1, 1997, <http://www.newsday.com/jet/year/cras1001.htm> (September 8, 1998).

Vincent, Stuart, "Their Anniversary Trip Was Going to Be Special," *Newsday* special section compilation, August 1996, <http://www.newsday.com/jet/jetbio1.htm> (September 8, 1998).